KEITH PIRT COLOUR PORTFOLIO

London Midland Lines Volume 2

Keith R. Pirt

BOOK LAW PUBLICATIONS

FOREWORD

The one thing about Tommy was that he was impetuous and quite often his brain went into gear long before the rest of him had time to catch up! So it was then, in the school summer holidays of 1959, that Tommy had it in his head that the end was nigh on the railways as we knew it and that he and I should therefore go on a grand adventure and visit as much of the London Midland Region of British Railways as we could - while we still could!

What Tom overlooked was the fact that we were only twelve years old! Not daunted by this minor point and blessed, as he was, with a 'Livingstone spirit of adventure' (something I put down to an over enthusiastic Geography teacher) Tom was determined that during the school holidays we would 'do' the London Midland Region!

"Tom, we're on holiday for six weeks not six months and my paper round only brings in a pound a week". But Tom would not be steered from his plan because by now the 'adventure' had become a reality for him. He was convinced that we could purchase a LMR Rover ticket which would take us anywhere we wanted to go for a whole week! I remember thinking, even at twelve, that if Tom thought we could get to Glasgow for that kind of price, then he had another thing coming. However, I knew better than to dissuade him when his mind was made up.

So, there we were, two fearless explorers on the bus from Stoke Heath to the railway station to buy our train tickets. We decided that the best time to go on our travels was the week before the Coventry holiday fortnight because then we'd be back in time for any Holiday Specials. I was whilst I was sitting on the bus preparing to buy the tickets for our momentous journey, that the little fat of being away from home for seven days suddenly dawned on me. "Hey Tom, we're away for seven nights, just a thought, but where we gonna sleep?"

"We'll buy a tent!" said Tom, and it was at this point that I began to have doubts and seriously wonder if Tom was taking that Livingstone chap too seriously! Now tents might be very useful in Central Africa but pitching one at the end of platform 3 on Nottingham Victoria would be a challenge even for Henry Livingstone or Stanley - I presume!

The second problem that my brain had now focused on was what were we going to eat during our week-long expedition? When Tom suggested that we ate in cafes, I then started to question the validity of the plan. Truth be told however, that by the time the bus arrived at Coventry station I was up for the whole thing. Whereupon we both purposely marched to the ticket office and Tom asked for "Two London Midland Rover tickets please". It was quite obvious from the outset that the booking clerk was not on the same planet as Tom, and had never heard of Livingstone or Stanley! His first question to us was "Where's your parent?". But, it was his next statement, informing us how much the tickets would cost, which effectively burst our bubble!

If at first you don't succeed!

Tom then made a minor adjustment to our original plan and announced that we would be better off doing the journey on a Midland Red bus! So, it was down to Poll Meadow to book a Midland Red Rover ticket which would take us anywhere in a day for five shillings. Before Tom doffed the pith helmet I felt it only fair to bring him back to the real world and point out that the ticket allowed us to go anywhere that was on a Midland Red bus route and that no, Glasgow was not covered, and, even if it was, since the tickets were time restricted, I doubted if we'd make that particular round trip within the margin.

A compromise it might have been but we talked and planned that trip with military precision and after Coventry Holiday Fortnight our duffel bags were packed and we were raring to go on our Midland Red bus - albeit for a tour around the Midlands! Well, I had a duffel bag but Tom had a suitcase full of jam sandwiches - so much for Tom's cafe idea! What a day we had. Nothing about it disappointed and it was to be repeated more than once over the school holidays which meant that by the end of three weeks' of spotting, we had well over 1,500 cops in our book and what we had seen was a very changing railway. The first signs of neglect had started to creep in and the lines of withdrawn locomotives were getting longer. There were the first signs of the green diesels but overall there was a serious air of change.

I have chosen particular photographs from the Pirt collection as I saw nearly all of these engines on that holiday with Tom and we visited many of the locations. The stored engines on the Winsford branch stand out as these were the first of the ex Tilbury 3Ps I had ever seen. They were also the last as they stood in the same line as the former North Western eight coupled tender engines.

I shall leave Keith to explain each photograph, although words are not necessary for some of the spectacular early evening shots. What I've tried to do is to select what a 'spotter' would have seen and not simply pick the rare engines.

Pete Waterman, London, 2009.

Copyright Book Law Publications 2009   •   **ISBN 978-1-907094-50-7**

First published in the United Kingdom by Book Law Publications 2009 • 382 Carlton Hill, Nottingham, NG4 1JA • Printed and bound by The Amadeus Press, Cleckheaton, West Yorkshire

A quiet moment at Bromsgrove station during a sunny April morning in 1958. Now this place was well within the range of the Midland Red bus services from Coventry but what did it have to offer Pete and Tommy. We are looking towards the famous incline (the gradient unmissable beneath the bridge) and the clear sky tells us that nothing has passed through here in the past ten minutes or so. Spotters were, if nothing else, patient and that virtue was usually rewarded with a plethora of traffic - well, nearly always. Bromsgrove was fascinating with or without 'cops'. The operation of the banking engines from start to finish was exciting to watch: the buffering up, the whistles, the sometime explosive starts from both the train engine and the banker/s, the determined, dogged movement of machinery against gravity, noise, noise and more noise. Besides the most famous banker of them all, 'Big Bertha' aka No.58100, we had the fleet of Jinties which served alongside the big 0-10-0 throughout. Then there was the LNER Garratt which hardly distinguished itself for one reason or another. Taking over from 58100 was another ten-coupled engine, the BR Standard 9F No.92079 and its sister helpers. Of course when this place was geographically removed to the Western Region a fleet of modern Panniers took over from the Midland 0-6-0T. In the diesel era Hymeks and...... - best not. That lot can be reviewed another time. In the meantime we are going to review the locomotive stock of the LMR in a sort of numerical order. In doing so we will visit some well known and some diverse locations. Hopefully we will 'cop' a few and be entertained by the quality of the photography - Pete and Tommy were. *BLP - M461.*

Ex LMS Class 3 Mixed Traffic Fowler 2-6-2 tank No.40063 presents a reasonable exterior, if you look past the recent accumulations of rust and road dirt, in this 14th April 1958 view at Bolton Burnden shed. The engine had not long since attended main works and carries full lining along with the new BR emblem but, almost before it arrived back at its home shed of Newton Heath it had been made redundant by diesel multiple units. Burnden shed had a surplus of siding space at this time (26A on the other hand was in the throes of 'modernisation' so space there was at a premium) and was given the responsibility of storing not only this engine but four other redundant Fowler 3MT tanks from Newton Heath. In the event these particular 2-6-2Ts never turned a wheel in revenue service again and eventually reached various scrapyards. No.40063 was not actually condemned until August 1962 - the last of the 26A quintet to be withdrawn. Truth be known, the Fowler 'Breadvan' as it was known in this part of Lancashire, was never popular with enginemen or the shed fitters, especially at the former L&YR depots. However, to our intrepid duo they were all LM locomotives which needed to be copped and counties like Lancashire had a lot of engine sheds worth visiting. Note the lack of sacking over the chimney. *BLP - M156.*

4

Resident LMS built 4P Compound No.41190 simmers in a quiet corner of Millhouses shed in June 1957. The 4-4-0 was by now just six months away from withdrawal and already its rundown external condition is doing it no favours with a ghostly sheen creeping over the engine. Its last shed (on paper anyway) was Grimesthorpe on the other side of the city but the transfer did not take place and it made the one-way journey to Derby works from 19B instead. The departure of No.41190 pre-dated, by just a few months, the change of regional boundaries when Millhouses became part of the Eastern Region and changed to shed code 41C under the newly formed Darnall group. The condemnation of the LMS built Compounds was now drawing to a close after a vigorous start was made in 1954, withdrawals carried on into 1955, 1956, 1957 and 1958. The few survivors that escaped into 1959 (some nineteen in total) could be found at outposts such as Gloucester, Lancaster, Leeds, and Monument Lane. Millhouses however managed to keep one engine, Vulcan Foundry 1927 built No.40907, under wraps until September 1960. Two others, the last ones in fact, Nos.40936 and 41168, lasted until 1961 although very little if any work had been performed by either engine for many months before their demise. *BLP - M282.*

Crewe works was a favourite venue for any 'spotter' and especially so during the heady days of the transition period when the place was turning out new steam locomotives alongside new diesel locomotives. In March 1956 this Ivatt Cl.2 tank, No.41288, had just completed a heavy overhaul after six years in traffic. A visit to the Paint shop ended its time at the works and it is seen posed outside that establishment wearing full lining and looking very smart indeed prior to returning home to Sutton Oak. One of the Crewe built examples (Derby only built the last ten of the 130 strong class) it did not fair too well after this works visit and was amongst the first of its kind to be withdrawn, a event which took place on 3rd November 1962. Its early demise most probably stems from the fact that the 2-6-2T was motor-fitted for push-pull working and that kind of work was rapidly in decline by 1962 either because the branch services, where such engines were employed, had ceased or because diesel railcars had taken over the job. The engine's final visit to Crewe was for breaking up. *BLP - M150d.*

Just down the road from where the Midland Railway's 'Old road' parted company with the 'New road' north of Chesterfield, was Staveley Works where British Railways employed ten shunting engines on behalf of the Staveley Iron & Coal Co. via a long standing Agreement (already well documented elsewhere). Amongst those engines were five former Midland half-cab 1F 0-6-0 tanks, a type represented here by No.41804 seen near the blast furnaces in June 1965. The terms of the Agreement drew to a conclusion at the end of 1966, after apparently being in force for one hundred years, but before then the ten locomotives 'allocated' to the Staveley job had been put into store as being redundant from 3rd October 1965. Nevertheless, BR could not withdraw or scrap the engines involved (Nos.41528, 41533, 41708, 41734, 41763, 41804, 41835, 47001 and 47005) until after the end of the century old contract. Variously stored at Barrow Hill and Canklow engine sheds, before finally languishing in the open near Rotherham (Masboro') station, the former Midland and LMS engines became the last of their kind and, ironically, the last steam locomotives in Eastern Region Running Stock. Note the front bufferbeam of No.41804 has a coating of what might be termed as Crimson Lake! *BLP - M21.*

During their headlong rush to introduce diesel and electric traction and eliminate steam locomotion, British Railways withdrew more steam locomotives than their main works scrap yards could deal with. Add in the factor that the Scrapping shop at Crewe locomotive works was being modernised and the inevitable queue is generated. The London Midland Region set up a couple of dumps near to Crewe where withdrawn locomotives could 'reside' until dragged into works for breaking up. One particular dump north of Crewe was created on the closed branch at Over & Wharton branch near Winsford, deep in the heart of the salt mining area of Cheshire. At its height, during the summer of 1959, there were literally dozens of locomotives stored on the branch, buffer to buffer. Amongst them were former L&NWR 0-8-0 tender engines which was no surprise as the location was centred within the former heartland of the LNW empire. However, what was perhaps surprising, and something of a magnet for hundreds of enthusiasts and photographers alike, was the presence of nineteen former Tilbury line tank engines such as 3P 4-4-2T No.41939 photographed in July 1959 - note the 33A shedplate still in situ! The Nasmyth, Wilson 1925 built 'Atlantic' tank was one of ten of its class withdrawn in that year which ended up at this place - far removed from Derby influences - to the initial delight of Pete and Tommy. *BLP - M362.*

It is June 1962 and still active on the West Coast Main Line - albeit on local work - is Fowler Cl.4MT 2-6-4T No.42378. The location is the climb to Morecambe South Junction and the working is a Preston-Carnforth stopping train. The Fowler Parallel Boiler 2-6-4T was probably the best post-Grouping design to come out of Derby, other LMS designs from the same stable are perhaps best forgotten for their inadequacies but this mixed traffic tank was certainly a success. Having only just transferred to Carnforth depot that very month, it was exactly thirty years old when captured by Keith Pirt's camera. No.42378 had started life in the London area working at Watford and Willesden sheds until at the war when it gradually crept northwards to Carnforth via the sheds located at Bletchley, Rugby and Stoke. Withdrawn 18th April 1964, the six-coupled tank would have by-passed Pete and Tommy's patch during its drive north but during its minuscule two week stay at Rugby in October 1957, it might possibly have been a visitor to Coventry station. *BLP - M43.*

Now, York shed was well off the beaten track as far as the London Midland was concerned. Pete and Tommy, on the other hand, would write off a visit because there would probably not be much in the way of LMR locomotives around the place - the LNER engines would have to catered for another day. However, a daily visitor from Bank Hall shed in Liverpool would show up in the shape of an unrebuilt Patriot or a Jubilee working a Liverpool (Exchange) - Newcastle (Central) express. Then there were various freight engines from Midland Division Garratts to Stanier 8Fs, all bringing and taking away freight throughout any twenty-four hours. Add in Stanier Class 5s from all points south and west, along with summer excursions to the east coast resorts at Bridlington and Scarborough and suddenly the count might seem quite reasonable. But, the presence of a Stanier Cl.4 two-cylinder 2-6-4T was not that commonplace, especially as late as September 1964. Keith Pirt noted that No.42548 was probably en route to its home shed at Newton Heath from a Light repair at Darlington works. Its external condition - clean - lends itself to the idea but Darlington certainly did not repaint the engine, especially the lining which had been applied a few years earlier at Crewe. Nevertheless a LM based tank, and a 26A (or was it 9D by then) at that was quite a sight at York in late 1964. *BLP - M293.*

Back onto LM territory, and Crewe at that, we see another ex-works product in the shape of Fairburn Cl.4 tank No.42151. The date is March 1959 and the Sowerby Bridge based 2-6-4T is at Crewe North shed during the running-in phase of its post-overhaul entry back into traffic. Built at Derby in May 1948, No.42151 spent all of its life working from just two sheds in West Yorkshire, from its arrival at Sowerby Bridge in June 1948, then transferring to Low Moor in December 1962. One of the early casualties of the end-of-steam-cull, the Cl.4 tank entered Crewe works in September 1963 for overhaul but was instead condemned and then cut up. *BLP - M54.*

Now here is a combination that was not observed very often. Stanier Cl.4MT No.42483 doubleheads an unidentified Stanier Cl.5 on a southbound express at Morecambe South Junction in August 1962. The Lower Darwen based two-cylinder tank must have been performing one of its last duties because the following month it was condemned. *BLP - M144*.

To finish off the sequence featuring the LMR 2-6-4Ts, we venture further north to Shap where, in July 1966, we see No.42665 running light engine near the summit, on its way back to Tebay, after another slogging match with gravity to help a northbound train on its journey. The tank was newly arrived at Tebay, its former home at Southport having closed the previous month. In April 1967 the six-coupled engine moved on again, this time to Low Moor but did not last too long there before being condemned. *BLP - M489*.

Nearly blotting out the bridge spanning the Chesterfield line at Dore & Totley, the smokey emission from 'Crab' No.42922 indicates that the fireman is putting a few rounds on the fire. The Burton based 2-6-0 is heading a southbound excursion, made up of Gresley stock, in June 1957; the adverse gradient through Bradway tunnel is coming up hence the firing now. Neither point of origin nor ultimate destination of the train is known but evidence suggests a Scarborough to Burton-on-Trent return excursion. *BLP - M16.*

Another nice mucky exhaust. This one marks the vigorous progress of Stoke based 4F No.44508 climbing the 1 in 100 through Farm Grounds, Sheffield, as the 0-6-0 gets away from the slow passage of Midland station in March 1958. The assorted freight train is bound for the Hope valley line, no doubt Gowhole sidings being its ultimate destination. *BLP - M31.*

The former LMS 4F 0-6-0 tender engines could be found all over the LMR but they could also be seen working over neighbouring Regions such as Saltley based No.44580 here traversing the former Great Western line through Fladbury on a crisp March day in 1963. By then of course this line was part of the Western Region and is still in existence as the main route to London from Worcester. The van train is headed for the latter place although its point of origin is unknown. Alas the station serving Fladbury closed in January 1966 whilst the 0-6-0 featured here expired in December 1964 at Saltley shed. *BLP - M44*.

As further proof of the versatility of the class, LMS Derby (1940) built 4F No.44598 climbs away from a stop at Dore & Totley station with a passenger train during a superb June evening in 1957. The train is a Sheffield (Midland) to Chesterfield (Midland) local, with a lightweight load. At this time the 0-6-0 was allocated to Westhouses shed and, as might be expected from a depot concerned mainly with the movement of coal traffic, was hardly looking its best. This duty was probably a filling-in turn for the 4F to get it back home - or as near to 18B as was possible. *BLP - M13*.

They did specials too. No.43953 heads the RCTS West Midlands Branch inspired Midland Locomotive's Requiem Rail Tour at Sheet Stores Junction on Saturday 16th October 1965. Starting out from Nuneaton (Abbey Street) station, and hauling six well filled coaches, the forty-four years old 0-6-0 proceeded on a 175 mile tour taking in main lines, branch lines, colliery lines, and goods only lines over the former North Stafford and Midland railways territory throughout the east and west Midlands. In the event, the veteran completed the tour, albeit arriving 30 minutes late, but the 200-odd souls aboard the special were lucky in being the last enthusiasts to be hauled by a Midland 4F 0-6-0 as No.43953, the last of its kind in service, was withdrawn some two weeks later, during week ending 6th November. Note the Midland box and LMS signals. *BLP - M389*.

One of the BR built Stanier 5s, No.44690, takes in the early morning sunshine at Rose Grove shed in March 1967. In the left background stands a reminder of previous motive power which dominated this particular depot's freight workings, the WD Austerity 2-8-0. Banished by the London Midland Region in 1965, the surviving WDs went to sheds in Yorkshire for further service. The one in the background would have come from Wakefield with coal for the nearby power station, a daily working for the 56A engines. The Class 5 was a bit a local lad having been built not too far away at Horwich in 1950. It first home was Bank Hall from October 1950 to June 1958 when a transfer to Derby took it onto the Midland Division. Six months later it was working from Leicester Midland shed but in March 1962 another move beckoned to the GC shed at Leicester. Just over eighteen months later No.44690 was back at Derby, this time spending over two years at 17A. It returned to Lancashire in March 1966 and made Rose Grove its home until the very end in August 1968. *BLP - M450.*

Horwich built No.44986 was coupled to this self-weighing tender, No.10590, from new in October 1946 to December 1963. The tender, also new in 1946 along with sister appliance No.10591, had a bunker which carried eight tons of coal whilst the water capacity of the tank was 3,750 gallons. The further building of self-weighing tenders was not taken up by BR(LMR) but those already constructed by the LMS continued in use virtually to the end of steam. This view of No.44986 was captured between Morecambe South Junction and Lancaster as the Cl.5 headed south with a fitted freight in June 1962. At this time the much travelled 4-6-0 was allocated to Mold Junction shed after a recent transfer from Dallam. In October 1962 the Cl.5 moved to Kingmoor from where, until its withdrawal in May 1967, it continued working traffic such as this. Before reaching Warrington in October 1960, No.44986 had started life at Southport, albeit briefly, prior to moving on to Bank Hall in November 1946. In May 1947 it crossed the Pennines to Holbeck and had three stints at that depot in as many years interspersed with similar residencies at Millhouses. Shortly after 41C became part of the Eastern Region No.44986 rejoined the LMR working from Holyhead. *BLP - M45.*

It was getting towards the end of steam in the Sheffield area in 1966 but some of the passenger trains, especially the short distance workings, were still occasionally handled by steam. A rather tired looking No.44888 (it was after all Trafford Park based) was seen defiantly working a Hope Valley evening stopping train, bound for Manchester (Central), during May of that year. Even after these workings were finished, the 4-6-0 remained defiant, moved on and managed to last out to the very end at Lostock Hall shed in August 1968. *BLP - M163.*

When this picture of Stanier Cl.5 No.45110 was taken at the terminal end of platform 6 at Manchester's Central station in June 1968, the engine was allocated to Bolton shed. The service on which the thirty-three years old locomotive has just arrived was not noted by Keith Pirt so we are at a loss as to where the train originated and how a Bolton engine was the motive power. Nevertheless, although some important points are missed, the picture itself is a cracker with a fairly clean engine inside the arched edifice which, along with St Pancras, was the ultimate in British train sheds. By now the once proud terminus had lost much of its traffic with the London services to St Pancras having switched to Manchester (Piccadilly) at the start of 1968. Only the Chester and Liverpool services remained and those operated by diesel multiple units. Less than a year after this scene was recorded, the station closed with the last trains departing on Saturday 3rd May 1969. The eventual resurrection known as G-Mex is a credit to all parties involved and long may the building survive but the mystery of that 'Black 5' alongside platform 6 in June 1968 remains. Somebody will know the story behind its appearance so please get your thinking caps on and write to the Publisher so that this writer can insert another piece into the jigsaw of railway history. *BLP - M320.*

With the evening sun highlighting the livery of the open wagons in its train, and the rust on its bodysides, Stanier Class 5 No.45254 (they did not come much dirtier than this) climbs away from Ais Gill viaduct with an Up freight and a tenderful of decent coal in May 1966. *BLP - M484.*

Just over one year later, and still on the S&C with the gorse in full bloom at midday, we see an unidentified Stanier 5 heading a Down freight across Arten Gill viaduct towards Dent station. Now, does this look a bit 'model railway' to you?. *BLP - M500.*

Another 'going away' shot but this one is taken on the Up side climb to Shap, at Hackthorpe to be more precise. Yet another unidentified Class 5 is doing the honours with a southbound express in July 1967. Note the LMS coach leading the formation. *BLP - M506*.

Just look at the length and diversity of the freight train behind No.44826 at Standish, near Wigan, on a warm June evening in 1963. The train was apparently bound for Bristol but the 'Black 5' (or should that be 'Dirty 5') would not be going any further than Crewe. Passage of the train south of Crewe would be in the hands of the Western Region with either steam or diesel haulage. The track would take it through Shrewsbury, Hereford, Newport (via Maindee North and East junctions), the Severn tunnel, then Bristol. The route of the freight is still in existence but traffic such as this, alas, is not. *BLP - M433.*

Birkenhead shed, March 1959. A very clean No.45440 is set up nicely for its photograph. The Class 5 had just returned from a month at Patricroft, which probably accounts for the clean appearance but not to worry 6C will soon have it looking shabby again. Virtually from new, this engine had spent its life working from Bath Green Park shed but twenty years later in June 1958 it was transferred to the Wirral when BR Standard Cl.5s took over its duties. A final transfer, in May 1960, took it across the river to Edge Hill shed where, in September 1967, it was condemned. *BLP - M526*.

Where it all ended. Carnforth - August 1968 - with Class 5 No.44781 standing beneath one of the two concrete built ash disposal plants at this historic locomotive depot. *BLP - M493.*

A wonderful picture providing food for those whose appetite for the lost summers of their youth is still sharp. The location is near to Colwyn Bay in June 1963 with two locals watching Class 5 No.44687, one of the two Caprotti equipped members of the class sporting the high running plate - half a BR 5 - was KRP's description. The train was probably the Down service of The Llandudno Club Train from Manchester (Exchange) which would have been traversing this part of the coast line just about then, according to the shadows cast by the evening sun. The train provided a fast service for businessmen to Manchester in the morning with an equally rapid return in the late afternoon. Both 44687 and sister engine 44686 transferred from Longsight to Llandudno Junction shed in September and April 1960 respectively and they became regulars on this service from their arrival at 6G until the train's withdrawal in September 1963. *BLP - M249.*

Smardale viaduct in July 1966 with another Stanier Class 5, albeit unidentified, crossing with a Down freight for Carlisle - it was difficult to get the views and the numbers. After all, it was only a '5'. *BLP - M193.*

There's not too much Settle & Carlisle in this album so perhaps we can get away with this view too. This is Ais Gill in May 1967 with Cl.5 No.44886 heading an Up micro cement train. Yes, it can be done - the view and engine number too. *BLP - M446*.

The impressive Chirk viaduct (yes we like our viaducts), situated on the former Great Western Railways' Chester to Shrewsbury main line. In March 1967 an unidentified Stanier Cl.5 heads south with a Chester to Wolverhampton express. Besides its situation near to the Welsh, English border, the viaduct crosses the valley of the Dee alongside the aqueduct carrying the Llangollen canal. To add further historical interest for the would-be visitor, Chirk Castle and the one-time border barrier called Offa's Dyke are all nearby. Even the railway station still functions, albeit as two modern stone shelters but nevertheless its still there! Don't forget the Glyn Valley to the west of Chirk which once had its own narrow gauge line to Glynceiriog. *BLP - M442.*

Back into the fields of Lancashire now and to one of Keith Pirt's favourite places alongside the WCML, just north of Lancaster. The date is August 1962 and Unrebuilt Patriot No.45543 HOME GUARD has charge of a Down express on the climb approaching Morecambe South Junction. The actual service is unknown but is could have been anything from a Manchester to Morecambe, Barrow, Penrith. Leeds to Morecambe. Preston to Barrow and Workington. Holiday extra, etc. The 4-6-0 had recently been transferred to Carnforth shed from nearby Lancaster Green Ayre along with No.45550. *BLP - M107.*

Not the fairest but, as far as Keith Pirt was concerned '...the rarest Patriot in this condition with the correct Fowler none-stovepipe chimney...' It is July 1956 and unnamed 6P No.45508 stands on the shed yard at Trafford Park receiving a water top-up. Soon to be disfigured however, with that awful stovepipe chimney which it carried to the end, the engine has worked in from Preston, a place it called home on an equal basis with Carlisle Upperby. The two depots virtually shared the engine between themselves during BR days. *BLP - M281.*

With the success, not to mention the apparent assured longevity, achieved from rebuilding the 'Royal Scots', the LMS decided to do a similar job with the 'Patriots' from 1946 onwards. They managed to rebuild eight of the class before Nationalisation whilst BR carried on the work until February 1949 when the tenth BR example, No.45522 PRESTATYN, was put into traffic. Our subject here is No.45532 ILLUSTRIOUS, climbing at the head of a Down express near Morecambe South Junction in August 1962. This engine became a 7P 'Taper Scot' in July 1948 and spent the next eleven years working from sheds in the Western Division. On 21st November 1959 it transferred to the Midland Division at Nottingham for an eighteen month stint on the St Pancras expresses. This was followed by a year at Saltley (obviously standards were rapidly slipping) until moving to Derby in April 1962. Finally, on the last day of June 1962 it returned to the WCML, working from Upperby. Just a few weeks later and here it is working homeward. With less than eighteen months of employment left before withdrawal, No.45532 must have put in plenty of performances like this because it managed to clock up the fifth highest lifetime mileage in the class. *BLP - M131.*

'Jubilee' No.45560 PRINCE EDWARD ISLAND has charge of a Down passenger near Preston in glorious sunny weather during September 1963. Note the carriage headboards! Having spent much of its life on the former Midland Division of the LMS working firstly from Holbeck, between August 1937 and September 1952, when it transferred to Nottingham for five years. A move to the Western Lines saw 45560 allocated to Edge Hill then, in January 1961, to Crewe North. This is the kind of work given to the 6P by 5A - lightweight expresses to Barrow, Workington or Carlisle. Rarely did the Crewe North 'Jubilees' venture into Scotland on passenger services but when they did appear north of the border, it would invariably be on parcels trains or express freight such as perishables traffic. Two months after this lovely evening scene was recorded, No.45560 was condemned and then broken up at Crewe works. *BLP - M46.*

It is late March 1958 and spring is in the air. Millhouses engine shed is now part of the Eastern Region, new code 41C. Other than the new code there was no apparent change to be seen. There was no influx of ER engines followed by mass withdrawals of LM types - nothing. Life carried on as before - no change. Unlike some years later when the LMR took over a number of Eastern Region depots - Annesley and Colwick especially come to mind - the indigenous ER allocation was decimated in favour of a mass immigration of Stanier products. Perfectly good locomotives, some only days out of shops after major overhauls, were condemned outright and sent off to LM works for cutting up. It was a raw display of corporate power and madness, not to mention a complete and utter waste of taxpayers - we owned the railway then - money. Why the culprits were not reprimanded in any way, shape or form was nothing short of scandalous and an insult to the public's intelligence! I digress. Grabbing centre-stage in the morning sun is 'Jubilee' No.45609 GILBERT AND ELLIS ISLANDS being got ready for a southbound passenger working, its Fowler tender topped up with the best coal Millhouses had to offer. This particular 6P, it may be remembered, had a nasty accident at Rotherham in 1948 but was repaired and put back into traffic. The next 'Jubilee' to have a serious accident was No.45637 WINDWARD ISLANDS, a victim of the disaster at Harrow in 1952, after which it was condemned and broken up at Crewe. The next 'Jubilee' was not condemned until eight years later, in September 1960. Its number - 45609. *BLP - M64.*

What wonderful names were bestowed on the 'Jubilee' class by the LMS in those pre-war days of the Thirties'. It was one of the delights of trainspotting to see the curved nameplate on a 'Jub' at the platform end or on a shed yard - 'just where are these places' went through your head or 'what does that word mean?' No doubt many a youngster involved with trainspotting would also be fairly good at school tackling the likes of Geography and British History. The imperial names of old had a much better ring to them than some of the latter examples put on by British Railways such as Pebble Mill at One, or a bi-lingual rendering of Some Cement Factory in Goodness Knows Where, for instance! This is clean and fully lined 'Jubilee' No.45629 STRAITS SETTLEMENTS, with steam to spare, awaiting the road at Euxton Junction in March 1961. Wonderful stuff. *BLP - M218.*

No.45629 has now got the road and shows off its long southbound parcels train. *BLP - M572*.

Besides the vastness of the Empire being recognised by the LMS, the names of British naval personalities, famous warships, battles and names with other naval associations were also cast in brass for all the world to see. 'Jubilee' No.45675 HARDY makes a pleasing three-quarter pose in Holbeck shed yard in May 1964. Note the absence of the lining which once adorned this engine and its tender. *BLP - M12*.

No.45586 MYSORE, looking less than acceptable, heads an Up fitted van train near Morecambe South Junction in June 1962. Having just transferred to Crewe North (for the eighth time) from Aston, the 6P had been pressed into service on a typical 5A 'Jubilee' turn. During the following August the 4-6-0 transferred yet again but only to Crewe South shed where it managed to eke out a living until January 1963. BLP • M233.

Now here is a 'Jubilee' working hard and looking clean too. Climbing past Millhouses, No.45572 EIRE presents a fine sight as it accelerates homewards with a Newcastle-Bristol express in March 1958. The 6P had spent all of its BR existence at Bristol Barrow Road shed since transferring there from Trafford Park in October 1947. Unlike most of the other Bristol 'Jubilees' No.45572 did not stay until the early 1964 'cull' but instead moved on to Shrewsbury in September 1961. It was transferred, on paper at least, to Willesden in January 1964 but was condemned that same month. *BLP - M325*.

Although we have preserved steam in profusion nowadays, scenes such as this are never encountered by visitors to railway centres. One reason why concerns the work stained appearance of the two engines illustrated - no self respecting group of enthusiasts would allow their particular pride and joy to get into such a state. Secondly, how many WD Austerity 2-8-0s are there in preservation - one, albeit not a former BR example - and that does not often rub shoulders with green 'Jubilees'. Thirdly, how many preserved locomotive wear that diagonal cab stripe? The location of this photograph is York North shed in May 1965 with Farnley Junction based 'Jubilee' No.45647, formerly named STURDEE, buffered up to resident WD No.90078. Evocative, atmospheric, nostalgic, terrific! Shed bashing at its best. BLP - M340. [David, this one is marked down as M344 but KRP lists it as *M340*.

As late as August 1967 'Jubilees' could still be found heading some of the Midland main line Anglo-Scottish expresses, mostly on Saturdays when Holbeck shed utilised their three 6P's: 45562 ALBERTA, 45593 KOLHAPUR and 45697 ACHILLES. This is No.45562 climbing past Millhouses with the last 6P 'Jubilee' working from Sheffield, a Glasgow (St Enoch)-Nottingham (Midland) service. Apparently most of the passengers on board the well filled cross-border expresses, especially between Carlisle and Leeds, consisted railway enthusiasts savouring - for the last time, many thought - the delights of steam haulage over the Settle-Carlisle line. It was reported that BR revenue on one particular service during August - the 10.17 Birmingham-Leeds-Glasgow - was up five fold! *BLP - M188*.

It is April 1966 and visiting York again, we find recently de-named 'Jubilee' No.45694, ex BELLEROPHON, mingling with green diesels in the North shed yard. The name has been removed but the 6P has been given one of the diagonal yellow stripes on its cab side. By now No.45694 was allocated to Wakefield of all places and made regular visits across the Pennines to Stockport where 25kV overhead catenary country was encountered, which was no problem for the 'Jubilee' but it was forbidden from working beyond Crewe - hence the stripe. Wakefield shed, which had been home since early 1965, were somewhat adverse to cleaning their charges, or so it seemed, so No.45694 mingled in with the 'locals' - the so-called Wakefield Pacifics aka WD 'Austerities'. The 4-6-0 was condemned in January 1967 and later sold for scrap. *BLP - M164.*

It is now near to the end for the 'Jubilee' class, at least as far as Crewe works was concerned, so lets have a last look at a clean member of the class in the works yard in May 1964. This is No.45626 SEYCHELLES shortly before it went back into traffic. Although a full repaint has not been applied (note the lining still in situ), attention has been given to the front end. After a lifetime working the Midland main line services, this particular 6P was evicted from Derby shed in November 1961 and spent the two years looking for a 'proper' home. It was sent to Burton-on-Trent along with a handful of its classmates but that was not a real shed, not for a 6P anyway. Then things took a turn for the worse a year later and it was sent to Annesley - a freight depot of all places, which had suddenly acquired a lot of passenger workings and required suitable motive power - indeed!. That residence was short-lived and during the first month of 1963 No.45626 returned to Burton to serve another year of not really doing that much. Holbeck shed still used steam, especially 'Jubilees' on a number of its more important services so when they required a replacement for a withdrawn engine they were given this 6P and to get it ready for more exacting work the 4-6-0 nipped into Crewe for a quick refurbishment. The overhaul lasted until October 1965 when No.45626 was condemned. At least it went out fighting and not in a whimper as would have been the case had it still been a resident of Burton. *BLP - M374.*

The setting sun highlights work stained No.45694 during that York visit in April 1966. *BLP - M343*.

Not wanting to leave No.45562 ALBERTA out of the reckoning, here is a rather nice one of the engine running light near Ais Gill summit whilst returning from Carlisle to Leeds in July 1967. *BLP - M492.*

By August 1962 the 'Royal Scots' had just about finished their work on the WCML - they were literally 'clapped out'. Withdrawals were about to start in earnest as the big diesels took on more of the work performed by these 7P 4-6-0s. By the end of the year the survivors were sent to other areas where lighter loads and easier schedules suited their seemingly fragile condition. Upperby based No.46108 SEAFORTH HIGHLANDER managed to see out 1962 but only just. Here in August the 'Scot' has charge of a Down express near Morecambe South Junction and appears in a reasonable external condition. From its entry into traffic in September 1927 until the end of 1962, and having spent much of its working life on the WCML, the 4 6 0 managed to clock up just over two million revenue miles which, by any standards, was very good. Amongst the first of the class to receive the 2A taper boiler, in August 1943, the engine ran without smoke deflectors until early 1951. Already stored after the pre-Christmas traffic rush, withdrawal took place in January 1963. *DLP - M112*.

Leaving Lancaster behind as it climbs towards Morecambe South Junction, No.46148 THE MANCHESTER REGIMENT heads north with *THE LAKES EXPRESS* in June 1962. The 'Scots' were another class which carried names to quicken the pulse, and get the grey matter working, with some really (to a youngster) weird spelling employed. However, the plates were educational to a point - what they did not convey was the fact that the British Army was much bigger than the few regiments represented by the class. And what was that GIRL GUIDE name all about? BOY SCOUT too! *BLP - M42.*

With six of the class withdrawn during 1961, the following year proved to be just as treacherous for the remaining half dozen 'Princess Royals' still working. In June 1962, with little other work on offer, class leader No.46200 THE PRINCESS ROYAL was given the job of hauling the Chester to Llandudno Junction leg of a Blaenau Festiniog bound RCTS special train and here we see the pioneering Pacific nearing the end of its journey and about to enter Llandudno Junction. *BLP - M371.*

Having turned, No.46200 makes its way to the 'coal hole' for replenishment. Llandudno Junction engine shed was not amongst those former LMS depots blessed with a mechanical coaling plant and had to make do with the age-old method of hand coaling, albeit occasionally with the aid of a small portable conveyor. *BLP - M25*.

Still replenishing its tender with coal and water, the Royal lady waits alongside the coal stage for the return eastbound working. Looking splendid, as was the usual case for special outings such as this, No.46200 appears to be a prime candidate for preservation but that, alas, was not the case. Stored for some time after its November 1962 withdrawal, THE PRINCESS ROYAL, unlike the other unfortunate members of the class which were cut up at their place of birth, was eventually sold for scrap to a company in Scotland. *BLP - M573.*

One of the two lucky 'Prinnys', green liveried No.46201 PRINCESS ELIZABETH, heads a northbound parcels train as it nears Morecambe South Junction in June 1962. *BLP - M41.*

(*opposite*) Going back now to March 1959, when subtle changes concerning the motive power, and everything else, began to take place on BR. It was a time when none of us really thought about the end of steam because it was still in fact being built. Admitted Crewe had turned out its last new steam locomotive just three months previously in the shape of BR Standard 9F No.92250 but that had not registered as a sign of the impending end. Normality was still in charge of events, or so it seemed. Locomotives were being condemned, as they always had been, but usually only after they had run the course of a thirty-year plus career so the 9Fs were good until at least 1985 and longer! We were at that time, so to speak, not prepared for the radical and drastic events which were about to occur. When the wake-up call came, as it had to Pete and Tommy, we did our level best to rush around trying to 'cop' everything before it disappeared. However, as Pete and Tommy soon realised, that to do all that we wanted to do would take time and money. School holidays and weekends gave us time and the most common form of fund raising - a paper round - was hardly going to give a young man from the north-west enough money for a weekend in Devon and Cornwall or a trip into the central belt of Scotland, never mind the far north. The overnight sleeping arrangements caused the most consternation, especially with parents, whilst the railway police and other officials did not take kindly to youths 'kipping' in waiting rooms, or on platform seats during the early hours of the morning, no matter what train you might have been waiting for. Luckily, various railway enthusiast societies catered for the majority with some reasonably inexpensive two-day sleep-on-the-coach excursions which took in a couple of dozen, or more, engine sheds in as many hours. Hectic and exhausting they may have been but well worth it. On Monday mornings sarcastic and seemingly sadistic teachers, immediately after waking you during lessons by throwing heavy objects in your direction, would enquire as to which part of Britain you had visited during the weekend. As punishment you could be told to write an essay about your weekend, describe in detail the area you visited or, "... and find the square root of three to the power of eight by first thing tomorrow morning..." as one particularly sadistic member of the NUT ordered this writer to do. His reasoning, now lost in the midst of time, mentioned my apparent love of numbers! They were good times - mostly. This is 'Princess Royal' No.46207 PRINCESS ARTHUR OF CONNAUGHT (on first encounter, a rather confusing name to a young man) outside the Paint shop at Crewe works. *BLP - M58.*

Now, does this engine appear to be in terminal decline or, does it look as though it would last forever? 8P No.46232 DUCHESS OF MONTROSE in full blown, lined Brunswick green livery. Once again we are outside the Paint shop at Crewe in March 1959. *BLP - M53*.

(*opposite*) No mistaking the shape of a 'Semi' as No.46242 CITY OF GLASGOW hammers through Euxton Junction with a southbound express in March 1961. *BLP - M24*.

An immaculate No.46225 DUCHESS OF GLOUCESTER at Upperby shed in August 1964, just weeks away from withdrawal on Saturday 12th September. Fifteen other 'Princess Coronations' succumbed that day leaving just No.46256 which was condemned exactly three weeks later on Saturday 3rd October. Rumours during the period between the withdrawals spread the word that No.46256 was going to be preserved but nothing could have been further from the truth. *BLP - M121.*

(*opposite*) Long before she became a celebrity on the post-1968 railtour scene, 'semi' No.46229 DUCHESS OF HAMILTON worked for a living on the West Coast Main Line. In June 1963 she was caught on film near Morecambe South Junction heading the Down portion of the erstwhile *THE LAKES EXPRESS* in what turned out to be the last summer when these magnificent engines were put to work in a reasonably clean condition, although that does not appear to be the case here. Withdrawn the following February, No.46229 did not take part in the final summer workings performed by the nineteen remaining though essentially doomed members of the 'Princess Coronation' class. *BLP - M217.*

In an effort to win over public favour by showing off their new motive power, alongside some of the old and not-so-old motive power, British Railways staged a number of exhibitions during the transition period from steam to diesel and electric. One of the venues chosen for the 1962 season was the former goods yard alongside Manchester's Central station. Centre stage, at least in this illustration was the penultimate 'Semi' No.46256 SIR WILLIAM A. STANIER, F.R.S. (the one with the longest nameplate in the class). Why No.46256 was chosen when the other modern, and more appropriate, 'Coronation' No.46257 CITY OF SALFORD was available or even the slightly older but even more appropriate No.46246 CITY OF MANCHESTER, is unknown. Other exhibits included the preserved Midland Compound No.1000, the latest 'Peak' and a blue electric from nearby Longsight. *BLP - M356.*

'We should just make Euston before it gets dark.' Might have been going through the mind of the driver of No.46227 DUCHESS OF DEVONSHIRE as it hurries an Up express through Winsford in August 1950. Photographically the railway cutting can be quite dramatic, adding further perspective to the scene but they can also, infuriatingly, hide the 'spotters' subject when approaching in foot but not quite within sight of the passing trains, just the residual smoke. *BLP - M99.*

Still at Winsford but during a different evening a few months earlier. We are now looking south at a very clean (perhaps ex-works) No.46253 CITY OF ST ALBANS heading a heavy Down express through the sun drenched Cheshire countryside in June 1959. All this would have been within reach for Pete and Tommy with their Midland Red rover tickets - just. But Rugby would have been their nearest call for spotting 'Semis'. They were after rarer fish and would be doing the sheds, main stations and important junctions, not to mention the goods lines with local fare. *BLP - M274.*

Looking incredibly clean for the period, green liveried No.46250 CITY OF LICHFIELD nears Farington with a northbound express in September 1959. The formation of the train appears rather interesting and it would be nice to know where that articulated set at the front originated from and, is that a Gresley brake behind that? *BLP - M133*.

To draw a line underneath our coverage of the Pacifics, and to make up for its non-participation in the Manchester 'do' we are including this view of No.46246 CITY OF MANCHESTER at Upperby shed in July 1961 when the 4-6-2 was still allocated to Camden. *BLP - M518*.

Leaving the glamour behind now, we take another look at the mundane, in this case the original Ivatt Cl.2MT No.46400 standing outside Millhouses shed in December 1959. Although mundane to us spotters' compared to their larger cousins, these modern 2-6-0s were well liked by both the footplatemen and shed fitters. BR were so impressed with them they brought out their own version in the shape of the Standard 78XXX class. Alas, like a lot of things related to steam locomotion at the end of Grouping and on into BR days - this class came too late. The first withdrawal within the Cl.2s took place less than eight years after the last examples were completed at Swindon. Ironically, No.46400 managed to squeeze in twenty-one years of service before its withdrawal in 1967. *BLP - M185.*

This is the kind of work on which the Ivatt Cl.2 excelled. Seen leaving Sheffield city centre behind, No.46485, a narrow chimney version of the class, has charge of the 0939 stopping service to Buxton in July 1966. *BLP - M147.*

Returning to Crewe works for our next subject, we meet one of their 'little helpers' in the shape of 3F 0-6-0T No.47505. It is May 1964 and the fleet of locomotives used for the internal shunting and shifting jobs within the works comprised almost entirely of these ex LMS tank engines. Our tank carries W10 as extra identification but in total some sixteen of these 0-6-0Ts were employed at the works in the latter days of steam locomotive repair, another less presentable member of the class hides behind our engine. Prior to these LMS built engines arriving in number, Crewe favoured a fleet which virtually consisted of former Lancashire & Yorkshire Railway 0-6-0 tank and tender engines along with a few odds and sods from other parts of the country. Somewhat ironically, the ex Lanky engines used to visit the works at Horwich for their overhauls. *RLP - M323.*

Williamsthorpe Colliery became the unlikely and final working place for three 'Jinties' towards the end of steam in the Midlands. This is No.47383, sans numberplate, brewing up magnificently at the colliery before commencing the evening coal train duties in June 1967. Besides this engine, 3Fs Nos.47289 and 47629, accompanied by ex LNER J94 'Austerity' 0-6-0 saddletank No.68012, were likewise working the colliery yard. Allocated to Westhouses engine shed for the NCB job, the work for the four tanks consisted bouts of waiting alongside the water tank at Williamsthorpe, interspersed by intensive shunting, short periods of heavy haulage from the washing plant to the BR exchange sidings, usually double-headed. That was followed by further shunting before returning to rest beside the water tank again. The engines worked in pairs on an apparent 25-day rota. It appeared to be the ideal job - the crews certainly enjoyed their time there. However, everything must pass, especially at this juncture of railway history. The Williamsthorpe job came to an end on Friday 6th October 1967 when an NCB diesel took over. The four 0-6-0 tank were withdrawn the following day and made history by becoming the last working standard gauge tank locomotives on British Railways. *BLP - M155.*

Another of the Williamthorpe 'four', Jinty No.47629, complete with smokebox numberplate albeit 'localised' in red paint presents a splendid sight in July 1967. All the lubricants were carried on the running plate for safe keeping, previous supplies having disappeared. *BLP M501.*

The Stanier 8F 2-8-0 virtually monopolised the heavy freight traffic on the former Midland lines of BR. Every depot from West Yorkshire to Wellingborough had more than a handful of the useful hard working and hard wearing engines. Westhouses shed was no exception and in June 1966 Keith Pirt captured No.48678 basking in the sunshine waiting for the call to the north-west and two further years of useful life. Before heading north however, this 8F had to do a stint at Colwick from October 1966, then it was off to Springs Branch and finally Newton Heath in December 1967. Its end came in June 1968 at the Manchester shed. *BLP - M291.*

Westhouses shed yard in June 1966 with 8F, 9F and one of the Williamsthorpe 3F tanks sharing the depot with more than a few Toton based diesel locomotives. *BLP - M302.*

A more distant view of Westhouses - from that seen on the previous page but also in June 1966 - showing the situation of the depot in relation to the surrounding countryside - coal country. The place was a typical Midland straight road engine shed with a ramped coaling stage on its northern flank and a large water tower dominating the west end of the yard. Modern disposal appliances were never introduced here by either the LMS or BR; it closed virtually the same as it had opened, only the motive power had changed. Although closed to steam on 3rd October 1966, the 0-6-0 tanks working the Williamsthorpe Colliery job in rotas, were serviced and stabled here until October 1967. By then the diesel motive power fleet which stabled here had grown in number, especially at weekends. Opened in 1890, the depot served as a stabling point for many years after steam had gone but as coal mining in the Derbyshire and Nottinghamshire coalfield contracted, so did the amount of work entrusted to the railway. Today the site is levelled, so relish this picture as pure nostalgia. *BLP - M466.*

To say that the Stanier 8F 2-8-0 class was cosmopolitan would be something of an understatement. From the initial LMS design of 1935 they emerged as the Government choice for War Department use in WW2 and were built in large numbers to cater for the requirements of all and sundry. The 'cheaper to produce' Austerity 2-8-0 then appeared and was built in even larger numbers specifically for WD use. However, the requirement for a heavy freight locomotive to work on Britain's railways existed throughout the conflict so the Stanier 8F remained as the first choice. Virtually every railway workshop in the country produced the 8F in varying numbers. The Southern Railway had Ashford, Brighton and Eastleigh turning them out during 1943 and 1944, Brighton managing eighty-five. The LNER likewise had Darlington and Doncaster produce over a hundred from 1943 to 1946. Another eighty were built at Swindon in 1943-45. Of course private industry was not left out of the mix and both Vulcan Foundry (1936-37), and North British Loco. Co. (1942) turned out dozens between them. To finish off we go back to the beginning. Except for twelve months of 1940, Crewe manufactured 8Fs continuously from 1935 to 1944, whilst Horwich were involved from 1943 to 1946. In August 1962 No 48443, one of the Swindon built engines, was working a Down hopper train near Morecambe South Junction in glorious weather. The Royston based 8F was hauling coke from Monckton Main to Workington, a reasonable journey by any means. *DLP - M111.*

Another Royston Stanier 8F, No.48067 in charge of a long train of empty mineral wagons, is seen passing through Mirfield whilst returning to the coalfield in July 1966. This engine survived to the end of steam on the enlarged Eastern Region and was condemned in October 1967. *BLP - M148*.

Now here is a pleasant though not unfamiliar location, far removed from what might be termed LMR territory. However, we think we can stretch a point with this one. Finding it hard to shake off the apron strings, Stanier 8F No 48412 climbs the Golden Valley near Brimscombe with a Gloucester to Swindon freight in May 1963. The Swindon built 2-8-0 eventually left the Western Region in July 1966 for Liverpool, first to Aintree shed and then for withdrawal, it transferred to Speke Junction depot. *R.J.P.*

Buxton was one of those out-of-the-way sheds rarely visited by most enthusiasts until the mid-sixties' when suddenly people started to notice that its allocation was essentially steam, fairly large and quite cosmopolitan to boot. It was hardly the most welcoming of locations, especially in winter when high winds made the cold feel even colder than it already was - a thousand feet above sea level. Not so long before this view of 8F No.48532 was taken (that is a red bufferbeam - apparently), Buxton depot, had a reasonable number of exLNWR 0-8-0 tender engines allocated. Now, just imagine working the winter months out of this place standing on the footplate of a G2 or G2A! One must always mix admiration with pity for the men who had to do that job for a living. By April 1967 the shed was still holding its Stanier and Ivatt allocation together and basically there was still another year to go before the stud of engines was either dispersed or withdrawn. No.48532 was one of those still in at the end for Buxton. It was transferred to Bolton from Monday 4th March 1968, the date Buxton shed closed, but it is unclear if the 2-8-0 actually made the journey to Bolton during the weekend and was then condemned at Burnden shed or was it withdrawn at Buxton before it even left? What is certain is that the 8F was built by the LNER at Doncaster by order of the Railway Executive Committee in 1945. In April it was allocated to Gorton shed but moved back across the Pennines and to Mexborough in December. Three months later it was back at Gorton but transferred to Immingham during the following June. It joined the LMS at Royston shed in March 1947 enjoying fifteen years hard labour there before crossing the Pennines once again and moving to Edge Hill in September 1962. A succession of depots followed with Lancaster, Patricroft and Newton Heath all vying for its services. In October 1965 it went to Buxton, enjoyed the fresh air and stayed - apparently to the end. *BLP - M304.*

Getting bang up to date now - July 1968 - with the end in sight. Carnforth, Lostock Hall and Rose Grove engine sheds became home for the last remnants of BR steam in August 1968 but right up to the last day the engines were busy hauling freight, parcels and passenger trains - no whimpering here. At Rose Grove the allocation consisted just two classes of engine by now, both from the Stanier stable and both extremely successful in what they had achieved for both the LMS and BR - the Class 5MT 4-6-0 and 8F 2-8-0. Illustrated here is a very respectable looking 8F, No.48773 complete with yellow diagonal stripe on the cab. This engine was one of the trio of Stanier 8Fs (48774 and 48775 were the other two) which entered BR service as late as 1957. No.48773 here was ex War Department along with 48774. Both had been built for the WD and then loaned to the LMS during WW2 prior to going back into uniform. No.48775 had been built for the LMS and was once their No.8025 but joined the colours in 1941 becoming at first WD No.583 then 70583. Coming back into Civvy Street, this lone 8F was not recognised by BR as being one of their own from LMS days, its former number waiting expectantly but needlessly. It was given a new number and a new lease of life, being put into traffic at Polmadie in September 1957. In December 1962 No.48775 was withdrawn at Polmadie but reinstated the following month. In June 1963 it was once again withdrawn at 66A but four months later Kingmoor reinstated it back to traffic. A move to the north-west of England brought it closer to sanity (of sorts) and a further lease of life. Its final transfer took it from Patricroft to Lostock Hall where it was assured work to the end. Like No.48773 here, No.48775 was withdrawn in that fateful month of August 1968. Note the 'industrialised' diesel-mechanical shunters in the background, one with a rather crudely painted 35 on its cabside sheet. *BLP - M167.*

Adding a flavour of the pre-grouping period, we go back to May 1958 and feature former London & North Western G2A 0-8-0 No.49115 standing in the shed yard at March with J15 No.65420 for company. Although right off the beaten LM track here, this part of Cambridgeshire was a regular destination for LMR engines, not only from the old Midland Division but also from the former Western Division too (remember that the LNWR had their own engine shed not many miles away in Cambridge). At the time of the photograph the 0-8-0 was allocated to Stafford shed but how it managed to get over to East Anglia is a mystery. All sorts of theories could be put to the test and somebody probably knows the answer but placing this particular engine in the middle of Fenland defies explanation by this writer. Much easier to explain is the presence of the J15 - it lived there, along with numerous others of its ilk. The former LNW 0-8-0 tender engines always appeared to be rather elderly in their design, indeed they were to a young lad in 1958 - perhaps designs from the emerging British car industry were having an influence. No.49115 was built in 1910 and looked the part. The J15 on the other hand was built in 1892 which made it somewhat senior to the 'youngster' from 5C. Longevity was on the side of the 0-6-0 from the start because in November 1959 the G2A was condemned and a few months later cut up at Crewe works. No.65420 remained in stock until 1st August 1962 - aged 70 years and 7 months! It was sold for scrap and ended up in the Great Bridge yard of J.Cashmore, right in the heart of L&NWR country. *BLP - M60*.

After our tour around the London Midland Region, and a few out-of-Region locations too, we end up in a quiet corner of Horwich locomotive works in March 1959, with former Lancashire & Yorkshire Railway A class No.52311 in the viewfinder. The 0-6-0 is not the oldest locomotive we have featured in this album, that title belongs to the ex Great Eastern J15 at March, but coming a very close second and certainly the oldest locomotive with a LM pedigree, No.52311 takes the prize. Built in November 1895, at Horwich, the six-coupled engine was visiting works for cylinder attention. A lick of black paint is still to be applied to the cylinder covers whilst the bufferbeam will also benefit from a coat of red on account of the new refurbished more flike buffers and wooden packing. Afterwards it returned to its home shed at Aintree and continued working until withdrawn in March 1962. KLP - M799.

Finally, and not wanting to seem 'pushy' in any way, this particular picture connects this LM album with the next Pete and Tommy 'adventure' - travelling the Western Region lines. Ivatt Cl.2 No.46519, trying its best to look 'GWR' turns on the triangle at Aberystwyth shed in August 1964. *BLP - M106*.